Ultraviolet of the Genuine

Hannah Brooks-Motl

The Song Cave

. . . for how could there be an inwardness, and how would it notice that it was one, whether as sorrow or as truly paradoxical joy, if it stopped being rebellious and desperate against everything given?

—Ernst Bloch, *The Spirit of Utopia*

The Song Cave
www.the-song-cave.com

Cover image: Orra White Hitchcock's drawing of contortions in clay beds, Deerfield, Massachusetts, 1828 (detail).
Design and layout by Janet Evans-Scanlon

ISBN: 979-8-9912988-2-7
Library of Congress Cataloguing-in-Publication Data has been applied for.

FIRST PRINTING

CONTENTS

STILL LIFE

The blueberries were wild, they were
Sharp and anonymous
Strewn creatively upon a platter near
The carcasses of duck
Destruction comes from seeds
That's common knowledge
When Word welcomes me back
To random layers glued together
Just beyond the legend's math
All the glandular changes
And things under the aegis thing:
    petty trinities
        colors   of poisonous sumac
      many summery zones
  All the general statements
    Shorelines and costumes
    Sandwiches, turrets
    How long will we do this?

ANTS

1

Autothysis sounds like
It has been around forever
Maybe Oedipus did it
Or one of the minor earth deities
Like Aristaeus
Tamer of oleaster
And maker of cheese
Fermenter, pickler, briner
Prowling a bijou maze
Of limestone and hive
In the era's ruddy
Inchoate logistics
Diversifying the flowering
Plants. I bet he had
A slender waist
Embraced his true
And commensal nature
Was right with
The optical flow
Or just occasionally
Hallucinated
Academically I've thought
About the idea
Of "origin"

But only as a metaphor
Could I have conceived
A bursting worker
And even then I'd worry
About explaining
Alienation. There is
A cherry tree in Marx
That I remember
Belongs to Feuerbach
Pull a single petal off
To wrap an ant in
A shroud not ungentle
Within the muzzy
Compagna

2

Autothysis
Was invented by a German couple
To describe a means of defense
In social hymenoptera: when confronted
By mechanical disturbances, the couple observed,
Female Camponotus saundersi
"Contract their gaster until it bursts at an intersegmental fold"
Whitish yellow and bright yellow sticky fluid results
Which traps attackers in the bursted thing
In the sacrifice of yellow
Elegies feel so opportunistic
Especially when there's cause to write one
Do you take a chemical cue
To the conversation
By the hill, in a pink moon where time is
A chemical conversation
Covering us with its fluid defense

3

One kills a bug now and then
But holds
Oneself aloof
And is quite perfect
Because death

Ants are hard to mourn
Though Sara thinks
They deserve more poems

Pretty globules
Smelly beads
Wonder-sensors

They came from wasp-like
Ancestors, their interactions
Have a rhythm
But no real meaning

And assenting
To all realities
Thus achieving
Magical effects
I heard a voice
The saying goes
Far out in front of me

Calling me
Solemn, mistaken
Actual, brief

It passed me on
To a particular zone
Blew my germ away

4

As one form of obedience to the human
Project, I note the beauty of words like *petiole*
Which could be a type of sugar
A cut of meat a folk dance or medieval refrain
The process of training something growing to climb
An edifice dynastic pergola the monumental sigh
My husband sighs proving effort
Has been around forever
It means their narrow waists
Of which sometimes there are two—two segments
Or a stalk in the plain world's enterprise
Waving beyond our sad visions
Of the violence about living

5

This other scientist
Conducts perturbation experiments
With her favored type
Returns to the desert
For an attachment is there
But nowhere in the literature
Do lovers peer at beings
As I peer into the soul of this
Pdf for its mix of styles
And lachrymose architect
Those two "people" in the
"night . . .

Of all the genres, grief
Is least avant-garde
A little slip of paper
Dipped in acid
At the mouth
Of the colony
These gathering densities
All upon the sphere
Swarming through
Your local forest
No one in charge

EXETER

In Exeter, England one June or July
we slept on the floor
Rhetorically, sentimentally—I bring
this up—
not to interpret roses or be watched
by the deer on Pulpit Hill Rd.
Yes it is strange
In everyone there is a certain no one
The garden, the blankets the poem
should be a world, a real world
Savaging the carved stone
Ymaginator
and the demi-angels now
just shapeless blobs
We walked along the river, England
Explanation implies a stubborn form of reason
strict materialism that narrows
the uncertainties
Maybe my clothes or my shoes
The cathedral in Exeter
The image screen
Everything I see, I see well
and long enough
One's lowest level afflicted with energy
corkscrew curls
flowing hair

dog by my feet
Maybe my clothes in the garden, on blankets
Mauled lump of limestone and this
rectangular boss
holding a covered chalice
or a story being told
about development
an ancient dialogue, at least since the 70s
Color would have evoked
unpain
notlack a texture to the day
lessrough and
useless in the charming, twisting streets
I don't want to be depressed by fake problems
so try to address them
in that great sand of past
Duty would have meant—
to be how the dog plays open, open
on a shield held by angels
bleeding at the gums
It deepens one, so seek it out:
St. Matthew is clutching a moneybox
Dead and lumpy
St. Bartholomew lofts his flayed skin
God or Christ
either the Virgin Mary or Christ
St. Paul flaunting a scabbard
and wearing a pouch
I looked at the scallop shell
& prophets wearing hats

But oh oh oh oh
I have pushed you down
in syntax for a thousand years
shot through with poison
Consciousnesss
used in the manufacture of cloth

ART IS NATURE

for Sara Nicholson

What's good for the codfish is good for the rat

What's right on the canvas bleeds into the myrtle

There are common bugs with no special status, I suppose they
incite one to question the composition

Juveniles pose by the hole of a vicious god and feed on
mums, ragweed, or horseradish

The chosen have fat diamond patterns in common but some
also lack this—they are cloudless, essayistic

Perched upon flowering legumes are false beetles, false
underwings, and the familiar bluet

Caught in undulating effort at being itself the damselfly flirts
with that prehistorical something

Can idealism ever be accurate?

When nature was dying and when art died too and the dewy
petal of the corn plant and virtues—

The heavy pollens, the bony fishes, the source of all edits

When no one knew the source of the edits

I blended right in with my poem

With imitatio and dramarama

The cold loamy lyrics exhorting this moment

Its partyers, parasites, radicals, losers, the brave

I give them a leafblowing nod

MARGUERITE: A BIOGRAPHY

Ronald Johnson
Loved his parents
Ed Dorn kicked his
Childhood down the road
Had it kicked
Both from Kansas
Of the Middle West
She called it
Marguerite Young
Wrote the Viennese
Philosopher, his wife
You need some perspective
I am so happy here
In New York
Maybe you know
The story of the poet
Who cleaned hospitals
Farmers read her work
Throughout the 1950s
It seemed the content
Of forever
Unremembered
But for the recluse
In their hour, this
"Singing at the door
For meat"—

Feel free of these
Associations
Or remain unmoved
On the subject
Of private stupidity
Its limits and obstacles
Why even suppose
Now I was afraid
It brought me in
To expression
Green Xs
And the word
Silver patiently
Diagonaled
In orange
Hanging now
Crystal in blue
My worthiest reading
Includes staring
At labor
Someone
In the woods
Of Wisconsin
Skims the Arcadia
Like a marriage guide

BERNICE: A FEMINISM

Died three times
Last rites twice
Never drunk or high
Served the goddess
Wrapped in a pond

POVERTY MOUNTAIN

Endure was her only name, she found it on the mountain
Our Lady of Fatima shining over there
and right here the shitty restaurant (Portuguese)
we go to any time anybody dies

At the intersection of all data
flowers
are keto to an energy healer on the phone
her small house in Detroit to convene
the fallen soldiers the paperwork
of poets upon some carpet
in a lounge

one experience of representations is there
in there or around and the boring depths
which mobilize what I do

Was It permissible
Who should Be firm

ULTRAVIOLET OF THE GENUINE

This is a story about phrasing
Being told on two levels

It has good bones, no bones—a minimum
Of advantages

It's got a garden path
At the height of summer, a little after

Pyramids of flowing pain
A window opens

Its latent layer
The songbook leaked

I still think it's powerful
A theory peaked

I think I was free there
Holding a goblet

One mutating afternoon
That's not personal, anecdotal

It just contributes
Whatever I say intentionally

That's about rhythm
I'll begin again

THE VASE

Do you write thinky poems or feely poems the painter asked
on the fire escape
Why should you consider me?
Thinky someone answered so guess it's true
I have a terrible imagination
That feels bad
Full of limits, the give and take
Of night
I walk within
A phrase-idea, the dusk
I'm standing at

Feely feels bad too

The objection to morals is they're too prescriptive, like
        What a palm reader said in 1998   a poet in 2015

All forms occur before the content of themselves   so time arrives
        by virtue of existing

from the outside   where a person never goes
Beautiful wild creature   who loves to read

Maybe it's just who you are—   yet an individual
cancerous and supreme   Or life's exactly

what every other poet said   a long green road
gravel either side and the feeling of

I have written that

That's all gone

Its lungs and mind

Then conversation shifted   and each gave their hierarchy
in the pantheon of artists
quarreling save for those   that concurred

in asserting the quintessence   of musicians, who
they claimed   irrefutably   reminded you
you are not dead   of which criteria they again

agreed to be nonpareil
to the kind of thing
the true artist   should aspire to achieve

I said I like ceramicists   for their beautiful utility
A vase doesn't make me glad to be alive
The novelist decreed

Hotboxing the minivan
Fries on the road

A woman far out
That anarchic spirit

At dawn
Another chorus

Lots of cans around
Paraphernalia

Everyone who went alone
Watching through the window

Their persons in the snow

These friends are not interested in your fine philosophies
There is a body   an urge that you deny   in order to
refine a proposition—?

You must join their tickled chaos!   but authentically
I still get excited when talk turns to art
Secretly I roll   around the word aesthetics

like a booger on my thumb
In Anya's garden out of Chekhov   like the middle
Of Gooseberries   in the pond, there was no pond

No man with a hammer but
a bird cannon   warning off crows from the corn
every 5-7 minutes   Is happiness thus

punctuated? Or woven as this idea I had   to call a poem
The Woven Head Piece in which, prosaic but inventive   bare
and intellectual in my reasoning   I'd move

from peg to peg in the overheating world
Bones of cows   discovered in brooks
Yards disclosing   twisted teas

All I can think is to think again
of the vaster partaking   of anything that is
the moms and dads   plus weirder relations

A chubby knee of which   we spiritually take part
Or belong utterly and to each—   the many of us gathered
on the fire escape   it was cooler there

I spoke of a gun range   at solstice
The definition of a firearm?   He told us as we ate
some feta   drizzled in honey

Tangled, sticky   in the old growth impossible
not to imagine   what's beyond the road, the green
so rotate the vase   to climb in

MUTTS OF AQUINAS

Nothing was plain or open, no one
was invited to explain Chained up all day
you might wonder: To whom does the good accrue?
Bad and good, says Aquinas
says Foot, are asymmetrical
We think he ate a lot of rocks because his teeth are worn way down
If you are defective in either X or Y goodness cannot be achieved unless
both are remedied
What kind of dog is that, the man would ask
He had no teeth then he had no shirt
or shoelaces
Good is thus harder and more than bad
the afternoon turned quick and functional
must be higher and rigorous in ways bad is not
She had a family but they were forced to move, due to economics
Looking into
the house from the side yard, seeing the nice arrangements
She carried her to the border and on the plane she begged
and begged
Will my dog be there?

A good man says Aquinas says Vollmann obeys all that is
rationally ordered but still can't count on heaven
Aquinas says Howe—who doesn't love to remember Aquinas
walking from town to town in Italy

he begat all kinds of thoughts
One should desire to live a marginal life   embracing constraint
and causing
little sorrow
With a feeling of mediocrity and vaguely outdoorsy
pleasantly the trees don't know us
or vice versa, even the past
forgotten and poor
No longer dallying behind, she stayed mostly by our side
pausing once when we took a wrong path
Stood to the right of the correct route, waiting for us
to realize our error

UNUSUAL FACTS

                    about oh anything:
                 Elephants may bury their dead, they seem to know them
and sing of them   Whales can be thankful
  The serpent forever rides our busy, mixy surfaces

I put a tick in a ziplock last week
                                                             in a sunbeam I
                     cut the struggling morsel free

then surrendered a notion at dusk by the pool
One should sit down with the beasts in semi-circle
                 terrible old circle
of rhododendron persisting after its first flower

                       Winking leaves of the American beech

WHEN

You're 90, 95 and living in the woods

Where fate waits

It's never been solved

When a person in the middle

Of knowledge, isms, supper

Moves from shelter to shelter, apologizing

There's snow on the air

When I speak of themes lodged at the foot

In the bank, on the rocks—

And think of the work

What I thought it might one day "do"

I think when did I think that?

Now I've lost some time in the early 2010s

Its heroic background stained with info, stars, water, and greed

Philosophical parables about going to the store

"I have exposed myself to the judgment of others"

Pools of wax within time's picture

Don't fucking tell me what to do

When considering an Aristotelian telos to life

I was a child at the lip of the canyon

When reason counsels something like—stay close to your defect

My friend fell from a tree, into soft mud

She was received

These concepts are emotional

Do not be afraid

And when this vexes our ambition

Attempt attempt attempt

Different zones of your mind offer resources, have you ever

Been offered a resource? That you need

It's fantastic

The alibis and asterisks, a little bit of screen

Prosperities and privileges and want

In that droplet when we were alive

Keep going + believe = "advice"

Take a seat at the waltz

Tend to the vulnerable and be consistent

Pull the scapula down your back

You have wings that need to open

It's a muscular effort but good

And for the many who ask will suffering ever end

In the Italian way you can say me I mine

A saint might call the long stretches

Habit or god or error

The veins

Of "the body" I put my nose in

Into the sensible essay of nerves

When everyone wants to deliver utopian energies

At the top of the driveway the author is given a halo

Medula oblongata

The pubes

To write of the dream having been to the place

The mortals who live on busy routes behind the golf course

Specifics, specifics

No substitute for the internet

Constellations scoring all our regard

In grids and rings beyond the encircling

This sick rock the maven crooned

I feel like geniuses advancing their explanations

Deliver strong deceptions

Imitating the worldly scramble

When teenagers are energized by thoughts of their enemies

When today is the day to organize the liberal poem of life

I liked the humanness of my feeble mind, the inclusiveness

Its weakness leant

Gizmos of man to remind us folly is real

And allowed to wind down, to waste the day

The crappy light

In that extra hour unsocial and getting wasted

Allowed to be

"A theorist of the personality"

When a child tore at their face

An adult was getting their shit together

When I saw an orchard, I saw a dog

We had shifted to the aftermath

With this cold gutted guttering feature

And a stack of notebooks

There's always some weird way to divest

THE SHIELD

I had a literary injury
Suddenly

An interlocutor
In my heel

As though
The hand of Mother

Still rested there
Squeezing and dipping me

In rigorous
Waters

In classicism's
Frail will

And an evil thought just
To my right—evil

Meditation
On the hypocrisies

Of a friend
Our small pious takes

In some proven place that aches
"Solid earth"

And coats the arrow
Of decay

I wish we lived like this forever, coming forth
In winter to antagonize the mind

A poet is a normal person covered in ticks
Now possessed of throbs and gnaws and stings

Robbed of understanding
Or robed within

All this hammering
That thinks

The rush of speech
The feel of rush no more distant than

The cities of events
Ergo primary nature

Which must be plain
And Pain

The dialogue you have there
Opening one's eyes

Coming back
From far away

BOWL OF FRUIT

Bitter is important to our bodies
I'm only interested in true statements now

Everything coming into contact with
the story is legitimate as well as bitter
and goes from mouth to anus—
chicory artichoke
citrus   red wine

Passing through this chain reaction
there are no false ideas

but we presume
the elegy, present the elegy
with flowers   asking where does it go
or looking at the spines
of books   a woman with short hair
holding a hand, and crying

someone bleeding through their nose   crying
they were removing a tube   then everything after

I would be lost without ideas
                              so I wander to the breezeway mentally
        in search of competent detail plus mystery
                stale and definite
                belonging somewhere

At the back of the tongue bitter activates bitter receptors
limited to a single act
traveling slightly diagonal through two lobes
getting smaller on the left
in the order of representations

Observe the rational animal

A table littered with plastic container
Great happiness next to the injury,
                                one slipped   By degrees
the gem might go floating away

An occasional habit
will never describe her unconscious as the patterns
          of English poetry are peculiar

          They remember
          an imitation

What we are left with

Where did all that wisdom go?

A yield of pleasure—pleasure for the living
vesicle pleasure for waking
waking the temples waking the liver

and a line of blossoms in icy rain
passing the car with clergy propped up in its
window

she carried and turned the many colors
she was running down

At odd moments I return
communicate poorly the meaning of events
the colors she turned against your cheek bending down
to say goodbye she vanished
was she pleased

a woman trying
to stand or shit leaking terror
and bitter from within ten thousand days
that won't ever be described

already manufactured by the liver
president
of an insignificant corporation
going from mouth to anus
passing into the actual beyond like a final idea not
clearly unfair

or fate deciding this chain reaction in a season of breaking
and the end of a world

One has the feeling
I'm looking back
on a bowl of fruit
like an image of utopia
meaning someone was among the whirl
arranged for it

The bowl is blessedly distant, it's getting close
The orange softens somewhat dropped
and placed back in again
into brownish hurt
a bitter greenish-brown returning
to some never determined main part

Could you argue with utopia's functional structure
that it gives research its vantage
that its dreams are so liquid
or nowhere's exactly perfection?

All right then. I don't need you.
I'll send you away. All right then.
I don't need this.

Do your dreams appear   with an o-o-o
          Are they imprisoned
                              in a tree

To tell this kind of story of hormone protein and energy going after
their freedom it's very distinct
To see the corpse that is our body
To turn away

            Beautiful private and severe as Vermont   regular people
        calling on history or their dead
            slow on wintry mix, on purpose   and not
filtering the bitter bad and good to give it all away

Sliding without prestige

All crying can simultaneously   take off
                                        and add to a face

                some wrinkled   reddened   new
but used look, newly used   by the tears—poor
face

The limit is thin: a moment of rage
at obdurate matter

You lay on the floor
Everything coming into contact with you

In pursuit of nothing
she rolled her eyes

her yellow yes
The world came down

the bowl pressed up
what fruit was left

POVERTY MOUNTAIN

a reference qua the epics
an evening
"coming out of my wormhole"
into the hollow
what's good for the scurfpea
to be like the soul
crisply transpicuous

MARRIAGES

First scenes of analogy, you're sucking me off
        In the midst of historical parallelism,   in the midst
                I'm rolling over   us naked alive
        poizing the scales of heaven
Look out and the leaves dawdle on snow etc.

Then comes some alliance: this bowl of cherry
        tomatoes   a little globe turning
rancid two from the bottom   conveys important truths observed
by Burke who could not recollect   any beautiful thing not
        also smooth

                The rancid smooth decisions
equidistant   from all ego, the era
        The inherited positions

an apartment's realism   on the river's struggle
    megachurch   on this watershed
      the fathomless rendition   reciprocating
 some genitals   in a book by Immanuel Kant

More parts of the union begin at the end
of Cuddeback trail pausing under some type of bough—
hickory? Elm? I put a mossing twig
a branched forked product
of time to mark the unmarked trail: there

Love revolutionizes, sure
Love the conduit of conditions
and world classics

Tenderly a hand, a shoulder, on on on
the eye mating environmental textures
this sprawling convention – cum – convenience
center that puts one in the field,

rooms with low ceilings and corridors corridors
communicating us to
the fourth part
of the fusion:

Inductive luminescence
crossing the highways of plenty
of nothing in that secret alteration
It's waving

A PINK CLOUD

A pink cloud clitoral hanging like a flap   in the upper part
of the sky . . .

There's Mariah in Florence
Alice James sitting in a meadow in her chair

I wish I'd been a philosopher or—   the wish
for philosophy   arrived late to me

Now these canopies arch   and they become
the question
resting by a square

INSTAGRAM

Just is-ing with the floral pattern in a westerly window here
Black fronds on the deepening blue   Our forward motion
into loss of course   misrepresents gain

And selfish oh the picture is there
Absorbing that   Which is the deepest chord
Funneling it away that's what it's for

Then in a clearish, peeish dribble—
Which is the deepest chord
Most worth upon our touching for?

Heading straight into the dry part of the spell
Without hurting anyone   I have a mood disorder and
my dog helps me   The burning agony

of childhood, adolescence
I was lost at sea, my dog found me
The simple agony   of aging and death

The irritating personal flaws
or menace inherent in certain invitations
I was sad my dog ignored me

Noisy buzzy night with your crotchets it has been
It has been forever since I wanted anything
experimental

POET DREAM

A published novel
A large recliner
Covered in thin red fabric
Very brutal
        An asshole geography
Like Boston . . .
The ones who didn't die righteously
Herons in the beans
        Picking their way across
        Rococoly

OMNIBUS

One's sensitivities
Can wander out very far
Heading to great imprecision
Eliot who loved Pascal
Who invented the omnibus
To prove that God exists
Also hated Montaigne
A gas, an infecting mist
Thomas said
The incarnation of doubt
An origin of personality
Who flatters and lies
Involves us all in meandering
The melting world
Of abundancing . . .

*

Voice is a prettily unhelpful term
First purple flower that lives a whole morning and afternoon
Dying in evening light—something voice would do
An ambivalence muttering and who wants
To accompany that?
But company it was
Over the hard brown ground
Petals, sounds

POET DILEMMA

Do I want seconds
I want to write a great poem
                    Here just falling asleep
Thinking of animal names   inventing
            a new way to do adjectives
     Sustain the regard, all corrupted parts
of the diction

Bananas crescent moons
there is rain and a virus outside they are falling
in a strange occasion the morning will be
"all mine"

Golden hills against the greyish truth   cemetery appearing
in the old romances   proximal, notational   sketchy

A teenager on main street, it can't be
simply impressions   yet impressive how the stars
                    arranged

Turmoils   the turgid passages
Luscious rash

          I have learned to say
from a long list of murders   such ecstatic personal austerities
     this great ensample
presumption and superior visions
               make up Art's heart

If you think words are made of poems
I mean poems made of words
As we're taught

I know plenty of words
Though I come from the provinces
Where the earth is filled with violence

Agentic, essential
To what is called the world
In high sun

A dark corner
Odd fog
In vital personality

Standing at the fair
I know dismay has some relation to lyric
Through repetition

And measure
Is a breathing castle
Stacking lines together

Science won't destroy our enigma
But does something to the glare
The peaks of these

Nodding grasses
Remind me of paradise
Where sentiment is hard and clear

POVERTY MOUNTAIN

The automata in a crazy way discovers the word I'm searching for—scree : so I pee beside the scree and reason all-form, each-use my voice in development.

Glove on a stick by the can of Busch Light along the rocky nowhere of this terrain of thought a little word connector word murmur image and feeling of consequence, generality of one woodsy grape so dilated it includes all variety of opinions takes a piquant elixir, appealing to the emotions : unruffled, aphoristic.

O beautiful accents of composite selves collaborating with analysis happily when absence can be pointed to—you have no mouth—you have not started to exist yet—abstract as two hairs in the book in support of hesitation a tidy hill with three kids smoking by the quality of rounded stones weather portion of belief in the green hand positioned by growth as though waiting for a stylus—dissolving into collective apotheosis fantasy to spread or extend to banish finally I'm replicating.

Purple Fiesta pulling up pulling out all of love much of shame that clear familiar place I would die even a college kid knew that, even though college. Out of an abundance. Some obstacle. Out of abundance and fusion, dead petals floating down from Heinrich Heine,

in bed one opening of Heine propped up against the chest and a certain page just fluttering out one secret to prosody I sought to love that secret first clear duration are we in it yet.

Elegant persons of a month ago unattended and clean valiant at restaurants/bars valiantly taking a swig child in a pink coat three dogs picking grasses saying you're a monster not a monster you're a monster repetitive slow beads of surfaced dew scaling blades of grass. Call someone on the phone take the disco to the meeting : where do you get your scraps.

I go to the mountain each day, have a dutiful dialogue with fallen leaves Pringles cans upon these wasted knuckles the beautiful kind repairing fictions eternity is coming take a walk with the outside the same mistake made in writing the same sentence as before. Same unit. Now fill the page.

Fridge around three am sounds like an ocean's inside semi-aquatic volume shifting against or upon the present buying yellow roses pulled back the trees deposited future to the soil said how it was with them it was April, April four everything behind doing predictable on a bad day on the z vector is that the one that comes right at you crawls right over I wanted to joke in bed with my lover we were in the middle of death I was dancing with friends they came along and we shoved. The lilacs were starting a warm and welcoming day all people out with their trials and joys I walked bare legged in a skirt smoked a cig people everywhere with their trials and we too sympathized it's somehow torrential and sad, the miniscule spiritual part ... finished Kyger's journal in the bath last night indulgent but maybe she'd approve the mix of gossip no it's just facts as they'd matter if you were trying to keep up who came over what they ate or drank Gary doesn't give her as good of presents no need to make commentary there it is kittens and lilies trying to vanquish taking a boat to worry about poetry—when—is it / it's not obscene pattern sounds so that new sounds emerge fully no slackness! a wreath swords few words adhered stone sky god yes and experiencing fury regular hunger I'm profound to this, this to me incorporated.

Renounce the basic premise the preamble pregnant prodigal the postdoc all haters and sentimentalists will never own this faculty the arrival of details remembered from the world : free love nudists holy beggars led by women in protest of avarice and tyranny all principles remade based on visions decades wars people don't belong there and yet it cannot but be—peopled speaking well, of comment.

Walk up the mountain there is conversation does it flow freely? A large too large to be merely vine hangs down little trunk inverted stop and marvel now a leaf goes right by gotta claim all the range : grass unmowed dandelions a few flowering trees the kind of place that might've been park just anyone's, everyone's, there. Consult the Madonna in the claw foot in the garden is the house properly abandoned rotten insidious urgency of ego smooth downward slope slick gliding fast bitumen a coating through the encounter where was I originally? Later it would occur

driving north in a poem practicing the names for time where the valley comes from it's our poverty so a kind of pity obtains a kind of violet outside god that mammal at night the edge of this milky garment as the daughter flees the times provoke some renegotiation. Was sleeping when the myth came up on my left the first era on the other side of age : ogre writing a whole book underneath this leaf saying it's a shitty time shitty to develop the language and stems! stems! stems! come, I'll find you a subject

"After the crystal became a closed system"
"Let the angels spin you in the air"
Life in a house that ruined the world
"Enough! or Too much"

Now of paragraph, at the edge of vocabulary ordinary important notions weak gestures opening the book placing the comma enjoying the sun in the sun now from the being or back to the being being within the being human-all or not little gold flecks—freaks—fully selved emboldened exposed on the rostrum ; assassinations murders dragged with hooks hermits and martyrs do not make a world in the promised sense, hostility survived dipped in the crime of politics and organism thinking everything's religion the biggest theology literally dusted off the bible just now googled Aquinas and Paul who prays.

In the training was taught meaning is immanent emerged a rose like a smell nothing above one gesture holding my hand position of bodies to contain something coercive walking down Ranger St turning left on Lorraine fairy lights spelling Hope on the fence names ensure the accuracy of talk metaphysics come in handy rarely but their trouble is constant, the very platitudes

Marie Tharp who first mapped the ocean floor unsung drafter for Maurice Ewing and his all-men she drew the trenches at the bottom of the sea have you had a marvelous biography?

Turning onto Tampa St at some point turning off the computer what did the minerals say the rocks that had been put inside to give us all to each other now I'm like humanity you too an evil stick by the slab. Average pleasure,

A poem with no research in it

Full of gait

That captured extant habits now it's silly a designation kind of communism for much of the night a new religion an hour north of Sacramento examination lasting many lines I stir it up, a confidence. Going into fog resident coming out changed faith wasn't happy in the fog came forward amplified gathering chaplets a sentence with my foot sharp on the red globe

where energies confer a friend a grandmother fire pit white cement buildings all of history asks why did you exist, read steadily through nouns—a golden quilt synthetic slippery cushions spread out to make a bed dogs children cars going in a circle why if I could bring paradise take a sip hold it in sit cross legged or on the floor and when you howl . . .

An area that had changed been changed a zone of conifers underwater deciduous trees their branches stuck way out over clouds. People walk through alive it felt like a living scenario where death forgot our future, waking up into that sensitivity remote strata browns and bright red but here a curtain's blowing in summer, a flowered curtain's advancing the single figure at the front of that at the end of that. Makeshift homegrown self-taught I'm getting presumptuous, confessing this :

nothing cures time.

Open the vents

DICHOTOMY

Purple cabbage flowers   broad leaves spill
somewhat wastefully, an inefficiency
supports   the   heart

garden friends on painted rocks
american spirits
woman in a blue shirt, black leggings   bleeding from
her head

POVERTY MOUNTAIN

there are variations
though I believe
in eternity
swaying untranslated
rude acorns
drubbing the roof
certain animals
awake in their bowls
a pit covered by water
old timey cabin
or shack transported
piece by piece
perched over
looking olive moss
golden Camrys
an imbalance
in concepts
niche
of the moment
ascended as a pilgrim
plateaued
the glorious way
I've huddled
against you
the government's

contradictory whine
if I name it
it's high over us
second to
jollity, gloom
and goes
to the monument
this kind
of order now
taking me up
beyond poverty
or the flag
ten years ago
in the autumn
months
the guardian
came over
the bridge
led by a little
King Charles
deprived on the floor
there's a place
beyond regard
stupid with quartz
sufficient
to all

POVERTY MOUNTAIN

Sleep in a field
Take off your clothes
Psychically
That's probably
What heaven means

Acknowledgments

For their ongoing, vital support I thank Ben Estes and Alan Felsenthal. I'm honored to contribute to the world of poetry, image, thinking, translation the Song Cave makes possible. Endless gratitude to all my friends who offered sustaining companionship and conversation over the course of making this book, especially Ingrid Becker, Peter Gizzi, Emily Hunt and Jacob Kaplan, Anya Klepikov, Kai Ihns, Patrick Morrissey, Gwen Muren, Sara Nicholson, Hai-Dang Phan, Jonathan Rajewski, Stacy Jo Scott, Allison Stephenson, Caitlin Spies, Scout Turkel, Caitlin Wick. Thanks to everyone in the ars poetica workshop at UMass spring '24 for your crucial insights, generously shared. Merci à Sabine, Pam, Katherine. Thanks to my parents, siblings, and grandmothers. To Lorine for staying with me the majority of the time. True love and thanks to Dan Bevacqua for absolutely everything.

Versions of some of these poems first appeared in *can we have our ball back, Chicago Review, Common Place, Cordite Poetry Review, NOMATERIALISM, Poetry Daily, Post45,* as a chapbook and in a poem sampler from arrow as aarow, a tissue paper installation created by Anya Klepikov, and in mailers organized by Kai Ihns. Sincere thanks to Michael Slosek, Luke Daly, Anya, Kai and the mailer crew, and all the editors and makers of these places.

During the years I was writing these poems, I worked full-time at Amherst College Press in Frost Library, where, along with much of Emily Dickinson's archive, the classroom drawings of Orra White Hitchcock are held. Many thanks to these women and to my colleagues at ACP and in the library.

The phrase "ultraviolet of the genuine" comes from Ernst Bloch's *The Spirit of Utopia,* translated by Anthony A. Nassar (Stanford University Press, 2000). Thank you to all the thinkers, writers, saints, and mystics I read and quote from in this book.

OTHER TITLES FROM THE SONG CAVE:

1. *A Dark Dreambox of Another Kind* by **Alfred Starr Hamilton**
2. *My Enemies* by **Jane Gregory**
3. *Rude Woods* by **Nate Klug**
4. *Georges Braque and Others* by **Trevor Winkfield**
5. *The Living Method* by **Sara Nicholson**
6. *Splash State* by **Todd Colby**
7. *Essay Stanzas* by **Thomas Meyer**
8. *Illustrated Games of Patience* by **Ben Estes**
9. *Dark Green* by **Emily Hunt**
10. *Honest James* by **Christian Schlegel**
11. *M* by **Hannah Brooks-Motl**
12. *What the Lyric Is* by **Sara Nicholson**
13. *The Hermit* by **Lucy Ives**
14. *The Orchid Stories* by **Kenward Elmslie**
15. *Do Not Be a Gentleman When You Say Goodnight* by **Mitch Sisskind**
16. *HAIRDO* by **Rachel B. Glaser**
17. *Motor Maids across the Continent* by **Ron Padgett**
18. *Songs for Schizoid Siblings* by **Lionel Ziprin**
19. *Professionals of Hope: The Selected Writings of* **Subcomandante Marcos**
20. *Fort Not* by **Emily Skillings**
21. *Riddles, Etc.* by **Geoffrey Hilsabeck**
22. *CHARAS: The Improbable Dome Builders* by **Syeus Mottel** (Co-published with Pioneer Works)
23. *YEAH NO* by **Jane Gregory**
24. *Nioque of the Early-Spring* by **Francis Ponge**
25. *Smudgy and Lossy* by **John Myers**
26. *The Desert* by **Brandon Shimoda**
27. *Scardanelli* by **Friederike Mayröcker**
28. *The Alley of Fireflies and Other Stories* by **Raymond Roussel**
29. *CHANGES: Notes on Choreography* by **Merce Cunningham** (Co-published with the Merce Cunningham Trust)
30. *My Mother Laughs* by **Chantal Akerman**

31. *Earth* by **Hannah Brooks-Motl**
32. *Everything and Other Poems* by **Charles North**
33. *Paper Bells* by **Phan Nhiên Hạo**
34. *Photographs: Together & Alone* by **Karlheinz Weinberger**
35. *A Better Place Is Hard to Find* by **Aaron Fagan**
36. *Rough Song* by **Blanca Varela**
37. *In the Same Light: 200 Poems for Our Century From the Migrants & Exiles of the Tang Dynasty,* translated by **Wong May**
38. *On the Mesa: An Anthology of Bolinas Writing (50th Anniversary Edition),* edited by **Ben Estes and Joel Weishaus**
39. *Listen My Friend, This Is the Dream I Dreamed Last Night* by **Cody-Rose Clevidence**
40. *Poetries* by **Georges Schehadé**
41. *Wings in Time* by **Callie Garnett**
42. *Two Murals* by **Jesús Castillo**
43. *Punks: New & Selected Poems* by **John Keene**
44. *ABC Moonlight* by **Ben Estes**
45. *Star Lake* by **Arda Collins**
46. *The Maybe-Bird* by **Jennifer Elise Foerster**
47. *Seriously Well* by **Helge Torvund**
48. *Dereliction* by **Gabrielle Octavia Rucker**
49. *Bookworm: Conversations with* **Michael Silverblatt**
50. *April* by **Sara Nicholson**
51. *Valley of the Many-Colored Grasses* by **Ronald Johnson**
52. *The Sphinx and the Milky Way: Selections from the Notebooks of* **Charles Burchfield**
53. *Telling the Truth as It Comes Up: Selected Talks & Essays 1991–2018* by **Alice Notley**
54. *Lunar Solo: Selected Poems* by **Jules Laforgue**
55. *Stranger* by **Emily Hunt**
56. *The Selkie* by **Morgan Võ**
57. *Hereafter* by **Alan Felsenthal**
58. *Cold Dogs* by **Zan de Parry**
59. *Saturday* by **Margaret Ross**
60. *Many Poems* by **Roberta Iannamico**